# INVESTMENT Terms & *definitions*

*A Glossary of Selected Canadian Investment & Financial Terms*



Investor Learning Centre OF CANADA

## Investment Education for People Like You

The Investor Learning Centre (ILC) is Canada's first independent not-for-profit organization solely dedicated to providing non-promotional investment information to the general public.

It was founded by the Canadian Securities Institute (CSI), the national educator of the securities industry for more than 27 years.

While information contained in this text has been obtained from sources believed to be reliable, it cannot be guaranteed nor does it purport to treat each subject exhaustively.

**Canadian Cataloguing in Publication Data**

Main entry under title:

Investment terms and definitions

ISBN 1-894289-03-X

1. Investments - Dictionaries. I. Canadian Securities Institute. II. Title: Investment terms and definitions.

HG4513.I63 1998 332.6'03 C98-932439-7

First Printing 1973

Revised and Reprinted 1987, 1995, 1996, 1998

# Welcome to Investment Terms & Definitions

This handy glossary of selected Canadian investment terms was developed by the Investor Learning Centre for the increasing number of Canadians who are taking charge of their finances.

The financial services industry, like any specialized industry, has its own language of specialized terms. In this glossary we have tried to reduce jargon, simplify technical terms and use clear, straightforward English.

In some definitions, certain words are printed in bold type. This indicates that these words are also defined in the glossary.

**At the back of this book is a list of other plain language publications available from the Investor Learning Centre. All have been developed and reviewed with the assistance of leading academics from the Canadian Securities Institute.**

# A a

## Acceptance Company Paper

Short-term **negotiable debt securities** issued by finance companies to fund loans to consumers for items such as cars and appliances.

## Accounts Payable

**Debts** of a company for goods or services purchased that must be paid within one year. These debts are listed as a **current liability** on the company's **balance sheet**.

## Accounts Receivable

Money owed to a company for goods and services it has sold. Payment is expected within one year. This money is listed as a **current asset** on the company's **balance sheet**.

## Accrued Interest

The **interest** accumulated on a **bond** or **debenture** since the last interest payment date.

## Affiliated Company

A company with less than 50% of its **stock** owned by another corporation, or one whose stock, with that of another corporation, is owned by the same controlling interests.

## Agent

An **investment dealer** operates as an agent when it acts on behalf of a buyer or a seller, and does not itself own title to the **securities** at any time during the transactions.

## Amortization

Gradually writing-off the value of an **intangible asset** over a period of time. Commonly applied to items such as **goodwill**, improvements to leased premises, or expenses of a new **stock** or **bond issue**.

## Annual Report

The formal financial statements and report on operations issued by a company to its **shareholders** after its **fiscal year-end**.

## Arbitrage

The simultaneous purchase of a **security** on one **stock exchange** and sale of the same security or an equivalent of that security on the same or another exchange which can result in a profit. The profit is the difference between the buy and sell prices and is usually a very small amount per unit. Arbitrage is a sophisticated manoeuvre executed by professional traders.

## Arrears

**Interest** or **dividends** which were not paid when due and are still owed.

## Ask

The lowest price at which someone is willing to sell a **security**.

## Assets

Everything a company or person owns or is owed, such as money, **securities**, equipment and buildings. Assets are listed on a company's **balance sheet**.

## Associated Company

A company owned jointly by two or more other companies.

## At-The-Money Option

An **option** with an **exercise** or **strike price** that is equal, or almost equal, to the current **market price** of the **underlying security**.

## Audit

Verifying the accuracy of accounting and financial records by a member of the Institute of Chartered Accountants. In some provinces Certified General Accountants and Certified Management Accountants may also act as company auditors.

## Authorized Shares

The number of **shares** a company is legally allowed to sell.

## Averages and Indexes or Indices

Statistical tools that measure the state of the **stock market** or the economy, based on the performance of **stocks**, **bonds** or other components. The **Dow Jones Industrial Average** and the **TSE 300 Composite Index** are well-known examples.

## Averaging Down

Buying more of a **security** at a lower price than the original investment. The aim of averaging down is to reduce the average cost per unit of the investment.

# Bb

## Balance Sheet

A financial statement showing a company's **assets**, **liabilities** and **shareholders' equity** on a given date. It shows what the company owns and what **debts** it owes.

## Balloon

In some **serial bond issues** a balloon is an extra-large amount that may mature in the final year of the series.

## Bank of Canada

The **central bank** of Canada, founded in the 1930s to facilitate the functioning of the financial system. The Bank of Canada issues and removes bank notes, acts as the federal government's financial advisor on **debt** management and foreign exchange, and conducts **monetary policy** to regulate the growth of the country's money supply and influence **interest** rates.

## Bank Rate

The minimum rate at which the **Bank of Canada** will make short-term advances to the chartered banks and **money market** dealers. Since 1980 the bank rate has been set at ¼ of 1% (25 **basis points**) above the weekly average tender rate of 91-day Government of Canada **treasury bills**. The upward and downward trend of the bank rate affects the **prime** lending rates that chartered banks give to their most creditworthy borrowers, as well as rates on all types of bank deposits, short-term **paper**, **bonds** and **mortgages**.

## Bankers' Acceptance

A type of short-term **negotiable debt** instrument issued by a non-financial corporation, such as Ford or General Motors, but guaranteed as to **principal** and **interest** by its bank. The guarantee reduces risk and therefore results in a higher **issue** price and consequent lower **yield**.

## Banking Group

A group of **investment dealers**, each of which individually assumes financial responsibility for part of an **underwriting** of a new **issue** of **securities** for a **corporation**.

## Bankrupt

The legal status of an individual or company which is unable to pay its creditors and whose **assets** are therefore administered for its creditors by a **trustee** in bankruptcy.

## Basis Point

A phrase used to describe differences in **bond yields**, with one basis point representing one-hundredth of a percentage point. Thus, if bond X yields 11.50% and bond Y yields 11.75%, the difference is 25 basis points.

## Bear Market

A market in which prices are declining. A "bear" is a person who expects that the market or the price of a particular **security** will decline.

## Bearer Security

A **stock** or **bond** which does not have the owner's name recorded in the books of the issuing company or on the **security certificate** itself. The holder of the certificate is the owner. **Interest**, **dividends** or any profits from sales are payable to the holder.

## Beneficial Owner

The real owner of a **security**. An investor may have securities **registered** in the name of a **broker, trustee** or bank to facilitate transfer or to preserve anonymity, but the investor is the beneficial owner and will receive any **dividends, interest** or profits from sales.

## Best Efforts Underwriting

The **underwriter** agrees to use his or her best efforts to sell a new **issue** of **securities**, but does not guarantee to the issuing company that any or all of the issue will be sold. The underwriter acts as an **agent** for the issuer in distributing the issue to his clients.

## Bid

The highest price a person is willing to pay for a **security**.

## Blue Chip Stocks

Nationally-known common **stock**, usually with a continuous **dividend** payment record in good times and bad and other strong investment qualities. These stocks are usually high-priced but have a tendency to be low-**yielding**.

## Blue Sky

A slang term for laws various Canadian provinces and American states have enacted to protect the public against **securities** frauds. The term "blue skyed" indicates that a new **issue** has been cleared by a **securities commission** and may be sold to the public.

## Board Lot

A regular **trading unit** which has been decided upon by the **stock exchanges**. For example, one board lot on the Toronto Stock Exchange equals 1000 **shares** for shares priced under 10 cents each, 500 shares for shares priced between 10 cents and 99 cents, and 100 shares for shares of $1 and over.

## Bonds

A **certificate** which is evidence of a **debt** on which the issuer promises to pay the holder a specified amount of **interest** for a specified length of time, and to repay the loan on its **maturity**. Strictly speaking, **assets** are pledged as security for the loan, except in the case of government bonds, but the term is often loosely used to describe any debt issue. Bonds are issued by corporations and by federal, provincial and municipal governments. Bond holders are first in line before **shareholders** to claim any of a company's assets in the event of **liquidation**.

## Book Value

The cash value of a business which, after all **debts** are paid, belongs to the owners of a company – or the **shareholders** – if the company is **liquidated**. This is calculated by looking at the **balance sheet** and subtracting the company's **liabilities** and value of **preferred shares** from its **assets**, and then dividing what is left by the total number of **common shares outstanding.**

## Bought Deal

An entire **issue** of new **stocks** or **bonds** bought from the issuer by an **investment dealer**, frequently acting alone, for resale to its clients. The dealer risks its own money in a bought deal, and in the event that the price has to be lowered to sell out the issue, the dealer absorbs the loss.

## Broadened Base Earnings

A concept whereby the **earnings per share** of a company are computed to include a **pro rata** share of the earnings of all unconsolidated subsidiaries and associated companies.

## Broker

A securities firm or an **investment advisor** associated with a firm. When acting as a broker for the purchase or sale of **listed stock**, the investment advisor does not own the securities him or herself, but acts as an **agent** for the buyer and seller and charges a **commission** for these services.

## Bull Market

A market in which prices are rising. A "bull" is a person who expects that the market or the price of a particular **security** will rise.

## Business Day

Those days when most corporate and government offices are open for business, usually any day except Saturday, Sunday and legal holidays.

## Buy-ins

If the seller of a **security** fails to deliver the securities sold to another person within a specified number of days after the **settlement date**, the buyer may purchase the securities in the open market and charge the seller the cost of such purchases.

# C

## Call Loan

A loan which may be terminated or "called" at any time by the lender. The loan is then immediately payable, with any accrued **interest**, by the borrower to the lender. These loans are used to finance purchases of **securities** and exclude personal loans extended by banks to its customers.

## Call Options

An **option** which gives the holder the right, but not the obligation, to buy a fixed amount of a certain **stock** at a specified price within a specified time. Calls are purchased by investors who expect a price increase.

## Callable

**Securities** which may be redeemed upon due notice by the security's issuer. In the case of **bonds**, issuers of bonds may reserve the right to pay off the bond before **maturity** to take advantage of lower **interest** rates.

## Canadian Investor Protection Fund (CIPF)

An industry sponsored fund that protects investors from losses resulting from the **bankruptcy** of a member firm. The maximum coverage is $500,000 per account, of which up to $60,000 can be cash. The CIPF is sponsored by the **Investment Dealers Association of Canada**, the Toronto Stock Exchange and Futures Exchange, and the Montreal, Vancouver and Alberta Stock Exchanges.

## Canadian Payments Association

This association operates a highly automated national clearing system for interbank payments which reduces costs and increases the efficiency of the clearing system in Canada. Members include chartered banks, trust and loan companies and some credit unions.

### Cancel or Change Former Order (CFO)

An order that cancels or changes a customer's current order.

### Capital

To economists, capital means the machinery, factories and **inventory** required to produce other products. To investors, capital means their cash plus the financial **assets** they have invested in **securities**, their home and other fixed assets.

### Capital Cost Allowance

An amount allowed under the Income Tax Act to be deducted from the value of certain **assets** and treated as an expense in computing an individual's or company's income for a taxation year. It may differ from the amount charged for the period in **depreciation** accounting.

### Capital Gain or Loss

Profit or loss resulting from the sale of certain **assets** classified under the federal income tax legislation as capital assets. This includes **stocks** and other investments such as investment property.

### Capital Market

This market brings together all the providers and users of **capital**, all the financial products, like **stocks** and **bonds** which make the transfer of capital possible, and all the people and organizations which support the process.

### Capital Stock

All **shares** representing ownership of a company, including **preferred** as well as common **shares**.

## Capitalization or Capital Structure

Total dollar amount of all money invested in a company, such as **debt**, **preferred** and **common shares**, **contributed surplus** and **retained earnings** of a company. It can also be expressed as a percentage.

## Cash Flow

A company's net income for a stated period plus any deductions that are not paid out in actual cash, such as **depreciation**, **amortization**, **deferred income taxes** and **minority interest**. Cash flow can provide a broader picture of a company's earning power than net earnings alone. Cash flow is important to investors as it shows the company's ability to pay **dividends** and finance expansion.

## Central Bank

A body established by a national government to regulate currency and **monetary policy** on a national and international level. In Canada it is the **Bank of Canada**. In the United States it is the Federal Reserve Board and in the United Kingdom it is the Bank of England.

## Certificate

An engraved document which shows ownership of a **bond**, **stock** or other **security**.

## Certificate of Deposit (CD)

**A fixed-income debt security issued by most chartered banks, usually in minimum denominations of $1000 with maturity terms of one to six years.**

## Class A and B Stock

Names used by companies to distinguish between two classes of **common stock**. Class A stock may receive cash **dividends** while Class B may receive **stock dividends**. There also could be differences in **voting rights** or in priority of **assets**. The investor should review the terms of the class designation prior to purchase to understand the rights of that class of stock.

### Clearing House

An independent institution that ensures the payment and delivery of **stocks** and **bonds** between **investment dealers** in a timely, cost-efficient manner. For example, an investment dealer may execute 10 trades (buys and sells) in the same **security** on the same day. Through the clearing house the dealer just settles the difference in the number of **shares** and the difference in money owed or received.

### Closed-end Investment Company

This is a company which uses its **capital** to invest in other companies. **Shares** in a closed-end investment company are bought and sold on the **stock market** and the company's capital remains relatively unchanged.

### Close

The last transaction price for a **stock** on a particular **stock exchange** at the end of the trading day. If there was not an actual transaction that day, the close can refer to the last posted **bid** and **ask** prices.

### Collateral

**Securities** or other property pledged by a borrower as a guarantee for repayment of a loan.

### Collateral Trust Bond

A **bond** secured by **stocks** or bonds of companies controlled by the issuing company, or other securities, which are deposited with a **trustee**.

### Comfort Letter

A letter filed with the applicable **securities commissions** by a company's auditor when submitting unsigned financial statements for use in a **prospectus**. The letter says that the final format of the statements should not be materially different from those attached to the letter. The letter is required because the auditor does not sign the report until the final prospectus is prepared for distribution. The signing is done after the securities commissions have reviewed the prospectus and any required changes have been made.

## Commercial Paper

Short-term **negotiable debt securities** issued by non-financial corporations with terms of a few days to a year.

## Commission

The fee charged by an **investment advisor** for buying or selling **securities** as an **agent** on behalf of a client.

## Commodities

Products used for commerce that are traded on a separate, authorized exchange, such as the Winnipeg Commodities Exchange or the Chicago Board of Trade. Commodities include agricultural products and natural resources such as timber, oil and metals, and are the basis for **futures contracts** traded on these exchanges.

## Common Stock or Common Shares

**Securities** which represent ownership in a company and carry voting privileges. **Common shareholders** may be paid **dividends** but only after **preferred** shareholders are paid. Common shareholders are last in line after creditors, **debt** holders and preferred shareholders to claim any of a company's **assets** in the event of **liquidation**.

## Compound Interest

**Interest** earned on an investment at periodic intervals and added to the original amount of the investment. Future interest payments are then calculated and paid at the original rate but on the increased total of the investment. This is really interest paid on interest.

## Computer Assisted Trading System (CATS)

An electronic trading system developed by the Toronto Stock Exchange that allows traders anywhere in the world to trade stocks listed on the exchange. This was the first electronic trading environment developed in Canada.

## Confirmation

Also called a contract. This is a printed acknowledgement giving details of a sale or purchase of a **security**, which is normally mailed to a client by the **investment dealer** within 24 hours of an order being executed.

## Conglomerate

A company directly or indirectly operating in a variety of industries, usually unrelated to each other. Conglomerates often acquire outside companies through the exchange of their own **shares** for the shares of the majority owners of the outside companies.

## Consolidated Financial Statements

A combination of the financial statements of a parent company and its **subsidiaries**, presenting the financial position of the group as a whole.

## Constrained Share Companies

Canadian banks, trust, insurance, broadcasting and communication companies have limits on the number of **shares** or percentage of shares owned by people who are not Canadian citizens or residents. Foreign ownership is restricted since these companies or institutions are either culturally important or fundamentally important to the Canadian economy.

## Consumer Price Index (CPI)

A major inflation measure computed by Statistics Canada. It measures the change in prices of a fixed basket of a variety of goods and services in the previous month. This basket of goods is supposed to reflect the average needs of a Canadian family.

## Continuous Disclosure

A **securities** issuer must issue a press release as soon as a **material change** occurs in its affairs and within ten days for any other changes in the company.

## Contributed Surplus

Part of **shareholders' equity** which originates from sources other than earnings, such as the initial sale of **stock** above **par value**.

## Convertible Security

A **bond**, **debenture** or **preferred share** which may be exchanged by the owner, usually for the **common stock** of the same company. Convertibles are attractive to investors as they provide the security and income of a **bond**, **debenture** or **preferred share**, as well as the opportunity to participate in the growth of the company through converting to common shares.

## Corporation or Company

A form of business organization legally created under provincial or federal statutes which has a legal identity separate from its owners. The corporation's owners – its **shareholders** – are liable for its **debts** only to the extent of their investment, which is called **limited liability**.

## Country Banks

A term for non-bank lenders such as corporations, insurance companies and other institutional short-term investors, none of which are under the jurisdiction of the Bank Act, who provide short-term sources of credit for **investment dealers**.

## Coupon

A mini-certificate actually attached to a **bond certificate** which represents an actual **interest** payment. The coupon becomes **negotiable** on the date the interest is due and usually represents the six month interest payment on the **face value** of the bond certificate. The term "coupon" is sometimes used as a slang reference to the interest rate paid on a **debt** instrument, i.e. the coupon of the new Government of Canada March 2015 is 8.75%. This means the interest rate is 8.75% per annum on the face value of the bond.

## Cover

Buying a **security** that you had previously sold **short**.

## Cross on the Board

When an **investment dealer** has both an order to sell and an order to buy the same **stock** at the same price, the transaction is allowed without interfering with the limits of the prevailing market. This is also called a put-through or contra order.

## Cum Dividend

This means "with dividend." Buyers of **shares** quoted cum dividend are entitled to an upcoming already-declared **dividend**.

## Cum Rights

This means "with rights." Buyers of **shares** quoted cum rights are entitled to forthcoming **rights**.

## Cumulative Preferred

A **preferred stock** which has a provision that if one or more of its **dividends** are omitted, these unpaid dividends accumulate and must be paid before any dividends may be paid on the company's **common shares**.

## Current Assets

Cash and **assets** such as accounts receivable and **inventories**, which in the normal course of business can be converted into cash within a year. Current assets are found on the company's **balance sheet**.

## Current Liabilities

Money owed to the company and due to be paid within a year, such as accounts payable. Current liabilities are found on the company's **balance sheet**.

## Current Ratio or Working Capital Ratio

Current **assets** of a business divided by current **liabilities**, thus measuring how much the value of current assets exceeds its liabilities. This is one of the tests to determine how much cash a company has on hand to cover its current liabilities.

## Current Return or Yield

The annual income from an investment expressed as a percentage of the investment's current value. On **stock**, this is calculated by dividing yearly **dividends** by the market price of the **security**. On **bonds**, this is calculated by dividing yearly **interest** by current price. For example, if the income is $50 a year on an investment with a value of $1,000, the current yield is 5%.

## Cyclical Stock

**Stock** in an industry that is particularly sensitive to swings in economic conditions, such as mining or forestry.

# Dd

## Day Order

An order to buy or sell a **security** valid only on the day the order is given.

## Debenture

A **certificate** of indebtedness of a government or company backed only by the general credit of the issuer and unsecured by property or **assets**.

## Debt

Money borrowed from lenders for a variety of corporate or personal purposes. The borrower pays **interest** for the use of the money and is obligated to repay the **principal** amount on a set date.

## Deemed Disposition

Under certain circumstances, taxation rules state that a transfer of property has occurred, even without a purchase or sale. For example, there is a deemed disposition on death or emigration from Canada.

## Default

A **bond** is in default when the borrower has failed to live up to the obligations under the terms of the agreement. Examples of this are declining to pay **interest** or **sinking fund** payments or failure to redeem the bonds at **maturity**.

## Defensive Stock

**Stock** of a company with continuous **dividend** payments, which has demonstrated relatively stable earnings despite poor economic conditions.

## Deferred Income Taxes

Income tax that would otherwise be payable currently, but which is not paid immediately. This is because larger allowable deductions are made when calculating taxable income than when calculating net income in the financial statements. An acceptable practice, it is usually the result of timing differences and represents differences in accounting reporting guidelines and tax reporting guidelines.

## Deferred Profit Sharing Plan (DPSP)

In a DPSP an employer makes cash contributions for an employee's retirement plans out of business profits. The contributions and earnings accumulate tax-free until withdrawn.

## Deficiency Letter

A **securities commission** letter sent to a company that has submitted a preliminary **prospectus** on a planned **new issue** of the company's **securities**. The letter poses any questions the commission wants answered, and outlines any recommendations for changes to the prospectus. When all points raised in the letter are resolved, the issue's final prospectus may be filed.

## Deficit

A financial situation for an individual, company or government where expenses exceed income.

## Delist

The removal of a s**ecurity's** listing on a **stock exchange**. This is done when the security no longer exists, the company is **bankrupt**, the public distribution of the security has dropped to an unacceptably low level, or the company has failed to comply with the terms of its **listing** agreement.

## Delivery

**Securities** sellers must deliver the **certificates** on or before the third business day after the sale. Delayed delivery refers to a transaction in which there is a clear understanding that delivery of the securities involved will be delayed beyond this three day period.

## Depletion

Refers to the consumption of natural resources which are part of a company's **assets**. Since oil, mining and gas companies deal in products that cannot be replenished, depletion reduces the company's natural assets over a specified time period. The recording of depletion is a bookkeeping entry similar to **depreciation** and does not involve the expenditure of cash.

## Depreciation

Systematic charges made against earnings to write-off the cost of an **asset** over its estimated useful life because of wear and tear through use, action of the elements, or obsolescence. It is a bookkeeping entry and does not represent any cash outlay nor are any funds earmarked for the purpose. It reduces the company's **fixed assets** to zero over a specified time period.

## Dilution

Reducing the actual or potential **earnings per share** by issuing more **shares** or giving options to obtain more.

## Direct or Indirect Holdings

These are the holdings of an individual or company in other companies. For example, company A owns 500,000 **shares** of company B's 1,000,000 **outstanding** shares. Company A therefore has a 50% direct interest in company B. Company B, in turn, owns 300,000 of company C's outstanding 500,000 shares. Company B therefore has a 60% direct interest in company C. Company A (by virtue of its 50% direct interest in company B) has a 30% indirect interest in company C.

## Director

Person elected by voting **common shareholders** at the annual meeting to direct company policies.

## Disaster Out Clause

A clause in an **underwriting** agreement allowing the underwriter to cancel the agreement, should a law, event or major financial occurrence transpire that adversely affects financial markets in general or the issuer in particular.

## Disclaimer Clause

**Securities commissions** require that all **prospectuses** carry a disclaimer on the front page stating that the securities commission itself has in no way approved the merits of the **securities** being offered for sale.

## Discount

The amount by which a **preferred share** or **bond** sells below its **par value**.

## Discounted

When some anticipated event such as increased **dividends** or lower earnings has already been reflected in the **market price** of a **stock**, it is said to be "already discounted" by the market.

## Discount Brokers

Brokerage firms that offer lower **commission** rates than **investment dealers**, but do not offer the services that investment dealers do, such as advice, research and **portfolio** planning.

## Discretionary Account

A **securities** account where the client has given specific written authorization to a partner, director or qualified portfolio manager of an **investment dealer** to select securities and execute trades on behalf of that investor. These are opened up as a matter of convenience to clients who are unable to attend to their own accounts through illness or absence from the country.

### Diversification

Spreading investment to reduce **risk** by buying different **securities** from various companies, businesses, locations and governments.

### Dividends

An amount distributed out of a company's profits to its **shareholders** in proportion to the number of **shares** they hold. A **preferred** dividend usually is for a fixed amount, while a **common** dividend may fluctuate with the profits of the company. A company is under no legal obligation to pay either preferred or common dividends.

### Dollar Cost Averaging

Investing a fixed amount of dollars in a specific **security** at regular set intervals over a period of time, thereby averaging the cost paid per share.

### Dow Jones Industrial Average (DJIA)

An average made up of 30 **blue chip stocks** that trade daily on the New York Stock Exchange. The DJIA is used as an overall indicator of market performance although criticism is periodically raised over how it is calculated, as well as the fact that so few companies are included so that it may not be a truly representative indicator of market activity.

### Dow Jones Transportation Average

Similar to the **Dow Jones Industrial Average**, this average is made up of 20 transportation **stocks** that trade daily on the New York Stock Exchange.

### Dow Theory

A theory of market analysis based upon the performance of the **Dow Jones Industrial and Transportation Averages**. The theory is that the market is in a basic upward trend if one of these averages advances above a previous important high, accompanied or followed by a similar advance in the other. When both averages dip below previous important lows, this is regarded as confirmation of a basic downward trend.

## Draft Prospectus

A **prospectus** prepared for internal use and discussion by the company issuing **securities** and the **underwriters**. It is not for outside distribution and shows only basic data on the company with little final detail about the terms of the planned underwriting. It is not a legal document and does not have to be drawn up strictly to **securities commission** standards. It is an earlier version of a preliminary prospectus and cannot be used in offering the security.

# E e

## Earnings or Income Statement

A financial statement which shows a company's revenues and expenditures resulting in either a profit or a loss during a financial period.

## Earnings Per Common Share

The portion of after-tax profits of a company attributable to a single common **share**.

## Equipment Trust Certificate

A **security**, more common in the U.S. than in Canada, that is generally issued by a railroad or airline to pay for new moveable equipment. It is secured by a first **lien** on the equipment.

## Equities

The stock, or ownership of **shareholders** in a company.

## Equity Earnings

A company's share of an unconsolidated **subsidiary**'s earnings. The equity accounting method is used when a company owns 20% to 50% of a subsidiary.

## Escrowed or Pooled Shares

**Outstanding shares** of a company which, while entitled to vote and receive **dividends**, may not be bought or sold unless special approval is obtained. This technique is commonly used by mining and oil companies when **treasury shares** (**authorized** but unissued shares) are issued for new properties. **Shares** can be released from escrow (freed to be bought and sold) only with the permission of applicable authorities such as the **stock exchange** and/or the provincial **securities commission**.

## Estate Planning

The process of planning the transfer of all personal **assets** at death to chosen beneficiaries.

## Ex Dividend

This means "without dividend." If a **share** quoted ex dividend is purchased, the investor is not entitled to an upcoming already-declared **dividend**. The seller receives this dividend.

## Ex Rights

This means "without rights." Buyers of **shares** quoted ex rights are not entitled to forthcoming **rights**.

## Exchange Fund Account

A special federal government account operated by the **Bank of Canada** to intervene in the world's foreign exchange markets and affect Canada's foreign exchange rate. Direct intervention to change the direction of exchange rate fluctuations is infrequent, and public economic policies are more significant in changing supply and demand for foreign exchange, and therefore the exchange rate.

## Exempt List

Large professional buyers of **securities**, mostly financial institutions, that are offered a portion of a **new issue** by one member of the **banking group**, on behalf of the whole **syndicate**.

## Exempt Market

An unregulated market for sophisticated participants in government **bonds**, corporate **issues** and **commercial paper**. A **prospectus** is not required to raise money privately from these private investors (largely institutions, but also individual investors) and registration of the issue with a **securities commission** is not needed.

## Exempt Purchaser

A category of institutional investors to which the sale of a new **issue** of **securities** does not require the issuer to file a **prospectus** with the applicable s**ecurities commission**.

## Exercise

The action taken by the holder of a **call option** if he or she wishes to purchase the **underlying security**, or by the holder of a **put option** if he or she wishes to sell the underlying security. Also refers to the action taken by a **rights** or **warrant** holder.

## Exercise Price

The price at which the **underlying stock** of a **call option** can be purchased, or the price at which the underlying stock of a **put option** can be sold. Also referred to as the **strike price**.

## Expiration Date

The date when **put** and **call options** and **rights** and **warrants** expire, as well as other privileges or conversion features.

## Extendible Bond or Debenture

A **bond** or **debenture** issued with a specific **maturity** date, but granting the holder the option to extend the maturity date by a specified number of years.

## Extra

Short for "extra dividend." A **dividend** in the form of either **stock** or cash in addition to the regular **common** dividend the company usually pays to **shareholders**. Also referred to as a special dividend.

# Ff

## Face Value

The value of a **bond** or **debenture** that appears on the face of the **certificate**. Face value is the amount the issuer promises to pay at **maturity**. Face value is no indication of market value. For example, a low grade bond may have a face value of $1000 but can trade at a **market price** of $130.

## Fails

Short for failed deliveries. It is the failure to deliver a **security** on the **settlement date**, or the date agreed upon when the trade was done.

## Fair Market Value

The value of an **asset**, under the assumption it is sold to a willing purchaser by a willing seller, under normal conditions.

## Fee-Based Accounts

Client accounts in which the **investment dealer** does not charge **commissions**, but charges a fee based on the value of the investor's account instead.

## Fill-or-Kill

A client order that stipulates that as soon as a portion of the order which can be traded immediately is completed, any remaining portion of the order not filled is cancelled.

## Final Prospectus

The **prospectus** which supersedes the preliminary prospectus and is accepted for filing by the applicable provincial **securities commissions**. The final prospectus shows all required information pertinent to a **new issue** and a copy must be given to each buyer of the new issue.

## Finance or Acceptance Company Paper

Short-term **negotiable debt securities** similar to **commercial paper**, but issued by finance companies.

## Financial Instruments

The term used for **debt** instruments, which are loans with an agreement to pay back funds with **interest**, or **equity securities**, which are **shares** or **stock** in a company.

## Financial Intermediary

An institution such as a bank, life insurance company, credit union or mutual fund company which receives cash and invests it on behalf of the suppliers of the cash.

## Firm Bid - Firm Offer

A firm bid is an undertaking to buy a specified amount of **securities** at a specified price for a specified period of time, unless released from this obligation by the seller. A firm offer is an undertaking to sell a specified amount of securities at a specified price for a specified period of time, unless released from this obligation by the buyer.

## First-In-First-Out (FIFO)

A method of valuing **inventory** which assumes that the first items bought are also the first items used or sold.

## Fiscal Agent

An **investment dealer** appointed by a corporation or government to advise in financial matters and to manage the **underwriting** of its **securities**.

## Fiscal Policy

The policy pursued by the federal government to direct the economy through taxation and the level and allocation of government spending.

## Fiscal Year

A company's accounting year. Due to the nature of particular businesses, some companies do not use the calendar year for their bookkeeping. A typical example is the department store which finds December 31st too early a date to close its books after the holiday rush and has a January 31st fiscal year-end instead.

## Fixed Asset

A tangible long-term **asset** such as land, buildings or machinery, held for use rather than for processing or resale. Fixed assets are found on a company's **balance sheet**.

## Fixed Charge

A company's expenses, such as **debt** interest, which it must pay and which are deducted from income before income taxes are calculated.

## Fixed Income Securities

**Securities** that generate a predictable stream of **interest** or **dividend** income, such as **bonds**, **debentures** and **preferred shares**.

## Flat

When the quoted **market price** of a **bond** or **debenture** is only the total cost of the bond or debenture, instead of the cost of the **debt** instrument plus **accrued interest**. Bonds and debentures in **default** of interest trade flat.

## Floor Traders

Employees of a member of a **stock exchange** who execute buy and sell orders on the floor (trading area) of the exchange for their firm and its clients.

## Flow-Through Shares

Tax deductions and credits, normally available only to a corporation, are given to the owners of the corporation's flow-through **shares**. Canadian exploration and mining companies are able to issue such shares at a **premium** because investors are considered to be funding exploration and development costs and are therefore entitled to deduct these expenses from all other income.

## Formula Investing

These are investment strategies. One formula involves shifting funds from **common shares** to **preferred shares** or **bonds** as the **stock market** rises above a predetermined point – and returning funds to common shares as the stock market declines.

## Fully Diluted Earnings Per Share

**Earnings per common share** calculated on the assumption that all **convertible securities** are converted into **common shares**, such as convertible **preferred shares**, convertible **debentures**, stock options (under employee stock-option plans) and **warrants**.

## Fundamental Analysis

An analysis of **securities** based on the fundamental facts about a company, such as sales, earnings and **dividend** prospects. This is in contrast to **technical analysis**.

## Funded Debt

All outstanding **bonds**, **debentures**, **notes** and similar **debt** instruments of a company payable after one year.

## Futures Contract

An agreement to buy or sell a **commodity** sometime in the future.

# Gg

## General Mortgage Bond

A **bond** which is secured by a blanket mortgage on the company's property, but which is usually subordinated to one or more other mortgage bonds.

## Goodwill

Goodwill is an intangible **asset** of a company. The buyer of a business is often willing to pay for the "good name" of the business in addition to the value of its assets. Goodwill appears on the **balance sheet** as the excess of the amount paid for the **shares** over their **net asset value**.

## Gross-up and Credit System

A procedure to encourage Canadians to invest in **preferred** and **common shares** of taxable, **dividend**-paying Canadian corporations by giving a tax break to such investors. The taxpayer pays tax based on grossing-up i.e. adding 25% to the amount of dividends actually received and then obtaining a credit against federal and provincial tax based on the grossed-up amount. This system is not available on **interest** from **bonds**.

## Growth Stock

Usually a non-dividend paying **common stock** of a company with expansion potential. The corporate funds that would normally be paid to **shareholders** as **dividends** are put back into the company to pay for expansion. Growth stocks have the potential for **capital gains** rather than income.

## GTC Order

This stands for a "good till cancelled" order. This is an order to buy or sell a **security** at a specified price, which is valid until executed or cancelled. This is the same as an **open order**.

## Guaranteed Investment Certificates (GICs)

A deposit instrument most commonly available from trust companies or banks requiring a minimum investment at a predetermined rate of **interest** for a stated term, i.e. one year, five years, etc. Generally non-redeemable and non-transferable prior to **maturity**, but there can be exceptions.

# H

## Hedge

A transaction used as a protective manoeuvre intended to reduce the **risk** of loss from price fluctuations of **securities**.

## High

The highest price that was paid for a **stock** during a certain period. For example, the high for the day was $80, but the high for the year was $120.

## Holding Company

A company that owns the **securities** of another company, usually with voting control.

## Horizontal Spread

Purchasing either a **call** or **put option** and simultaneously selling the same type of option with the same **strike price** but a different expiration month.

## Hypothecate

To pledge **securities** as **collateral** for a loan.

# I

## If, as and when

Indicates a conditional transaction in a **security** that is authorized for issuance, but not issued yet. New **primary offerings** can trade on an "if, as and when" issued basis prior to listing on an exchange.

## In-and-Out

The purchase and sale of the same **security** within a short period of time, usually a day, week or month. An in-and-out trader is more interested in profiting from day-to-day price fluctuations than in receiving **dividends** or long-term growth.

## In-The-Money Option

A **call option** is in-the-money if its **exercise** or **strike price** is below the current **market price** of the **underlying stock**. A **put option** is in-the-money if its strike price is above the current market price of the underlying stock.

## Income Bond

Generally, an income bond promises to repay **principal** but only to pay **interest** when the company earns a certain amount of money. In some cases, if the interest is unpaid on an income bond, it may accumulate as a claim against the company when the bond matures.

## Income Stock

A **common stock** that pays, or is expected to pay, an attractive **dividend** to **shareholders**. Usually stock from a more mature company that does not expect expansion or growth – therefore money is not required internally for equipment, etc.

## Index or Average

A statistical tool that measures the state of the **stock market** or the economy, based on the performance of **stocks** or other meaningful components. Examples are the **TSE 300 Composite Index**, The Montreal Exchange Market Portfolio Index and the **Dow Jones Industrial Average**.

## Insider

Directors, senior officers and any other people, such as lawyers and accountants, who can be presumed to have access to non-public information concerning a company. It also includes anyone owning more than 10% of the voting **shares** in a corporation.

## Insider Report

A report of all transactions in the **shares** of a company made by those considered to be **insiders** of the company. It is submitted each month to the provincial **securities commissions** and allows the administrators to monitor trading by such people to ensure regulations are not violated.

## Installment Debentures

A **bond** or **debenture issue** in which a predetermined amount of the **principal** becomes due and payable each year. Also called a **serial bond or debenture**. This is popular as a municipal financing vehicle.

## Installment Receipts

A **new issue** of **stock** sold with the obligation that buyers will pay the issue price in a series of installment payments instead of one lump sum payment. This is also known as partially paid shares. The buyer usually pays a deposit upon settlement, perhaps one-half the issue price of the shares, with the balance to be paid in one year.

## Institutional Clients

The sales department of a securities firm serves two categories of clients. The institutional segment deals with banks, insurance companies, trust companies, pension fund managers and large corporations. The retail branch deals with individual investors.

## Intangible Asset

An **asset** which has no physical substance, such as **goodwill**, patents, trademarks and copyrights.

## Interest

Money charged by a lender to a borrower for the use of his or her money.

## Interim Certificates

When a **new issue** of a **security** is marketed, temporary **certificates**, called interim certificates, are sometimes delivered. These are later exchanged for permanent or definitive certificates.

## Interim Statements

These are financial statements issued for a certain period within a fiscal year, such as a three-month or first quarter interim statement.

## Intrinsic Value

That portion of a **warrant**, **right** or **call option**'s price that represents the amount by which the **market price** of the **underlying security** exceeds the price at which the warrant, right or call option may be **exercised**. The intrinsic value of a **put** is calculated as the amount by which the underlying security's market value is below the price at which the put option can be exercised.

## Inventory

For most companies this is merchandise, raw materials, unfinished products and finished products of a business that have not yet been sold. **Investment dealers** hold inventories of **shares**, **bonds**, **debentures** and other investment products to fill **long** and **short** positions for clients.

## Inventory Turnover Ratio

This is the cost of goods sold by a company, divided by its **inventory**. The ratio may also be expressed in terms of the number of days required to sell current inventory by dividing the ratio into 365. This ratio indicates the efficiency of management in turning over the company's inventory and can be used to compare with other companies in the same field.

## Investment

The purchase or ownership of a **security** to make money by gaining income, increasing **capital**, or both. Investments may also include artwork, antiques and real estate.

## Investment Advisor

This is a person employed by an **investment dealer** who provides investment advice to clients and executes trades on their behalf in **securities** and other investment products. Investment advisors must attain set educational qualifications, follow certain rules and regulations and be registered by the **securities commission** in the province in which he or she works.

## Investment Counsellor

A specialist in the investment industry paid by fee to provide advice and research to investors with larger sized accounts.

## Investment Dealer

This refers to securities firms which employ investment advisors to work with retail and **institutional clients** and has **underwriting**, trading and research departments.

## Investment Dealers Association of Canada (IDA)

The Canadian investment industry's national trade association and **self-regulatory organization**. The IDA represents and polices the activities of approximately 114 member firms.

## Investor

A person whose principal concern in the purchase of a **security** is the minimizing of **risk**, compared to the **speculator** who is prepared to accept calculated risk in the hope of making better-than-average profits, or the "gambler" who is prepared to take even greater risks. More generally it refers to people who invest money in investment products.

## Issue

Any of a company's **securities**, or the act of distributing them. Issued shares refer to that part of the **authorized shares** which have been issued for sale by the corporation. The total number of authorized shares does not have to be issued.

## Issuer Bid

An offer by an issuer to buy back some of its own **securities**. This is usually done because the company feels the market is undervaluing its securities.

# J

## Jitney

The execution and clearing of orders by one member of a **stock exchange** for the account of another member. For example, **investment dealer** A is a small firm whose volume of business is not sufficient to maintain a **trader** on the exchange. Instead it gives its orders to investment dealer B for execution and pays a reduced percentage of the normal **commission**.

## Junior Bond Issue

A corporate **bond issue**, the **collateral** for which has been pledged as **security** for other more senior **debt** issues, and therefore ranks behind these prior claims.

## Junior Debt

One or more **junior bond issues**.

## Lagging Indicators

These are market indicators that often continue an upward trend after the peak of the economy has been signalled by other economic indicators – or continue a downward trend after a rise has been signalled. These indicators include business expenditures for new plants and equipment, consumers' installment credit, short-term business loans and the overall value of manufacturing and trade inventories. For example, it is often difficult to cancel contracts on short notice, so although sales have slowed for a retail store, the business cannot refuse supplies ordered prior to the downturn, but delivered after the peak in sales. These lagging indicators can confirm or deny the trend shown by the **leading indicators**.

## Last-In-First-Out (LIFO)

A method of valuing **inventory** which assumes that the last articles bought are the first used or sold.

## Leading Indicators

These are market indicators that usually move before the general economy changes direction. Such indicators include employment, profits and certain **commodity** prices. For example, business profits start to rise during an economic expansion, but as the economy reaches the peak the rate at which profits increase slows down. Profits begin to flatten out and decrease as employment costs increase (caused by overtime needed to meet high demand) and cut into profit margins. At the peak of the economy, profits already are beginning to fall. Therefore profits lead the general economy and give some warning of economic conditions to come.

## Legal Investment

In some provinces the law requires that a **trustee** may only invest funds in a list of **securities** designated by the province or the federal government.

## Leverage

The effect of **fixed charges** such as **debt interest** or **preferred dividends** on per-share earnings of **common stock**. Increases or decreases in income before fixed charges result in magnified percentage increases or decreases in **earnings per common share**. Leverage also applies to seeking magnified percentage returns on an investment by using borrowed funds, **margin accounts** or buying **securities** which require payment of only a fraction of the **underlying** security's value, such as **rights**, **warrants** or **options**.

## Leveraged Buy Out (LBO)

A **takeover** financed to a large degree by **debt** that is secured, serviced and repaid through the cash flow and **assets** of the acquired company. Typically, an LBO is financed predominantly by bank debt and low quality **bonds**, and to a minimum degree by **equity**. Its extreme **leverage** makes an LBO dependent upon a stable economy and stable **interest** rates, as well as a stable **cash flow** from the acquired company for its success.

## Liabilities

These are the **debts** and obligations of a company. Current liabilities are debts due and payable within one year. Long-term liabilities are those payable after one year. Liabilities are found on a company's **balance sheet**.

## Lien

This is the claim against property pledged or **mortgaged** to secure performance of an obligation.

## Life Annuity

A contract which guarantees the planholder a regular monthly income for life in exchange for an amount of money in a **Registered Retirement Savings Plan (RRSP)**.

## Limit Order

This is a client's order to buy or sell a **security** at a specific price. The order can be executed only at that price or a better one. It sets the maximum price the client is willing to pay as a buyer, and the minimum price he or she is willing to accept as a seller.

## Limited Liability

When "limited" is at the end of a Canadian company's name, the company's **shareholders**' responsibility for the **debts** of the company is limited to the amount of money they paid to buy the **shares**. In contrast, ownership of a company by a sole proprietor or partnership carries unlimited personal legal responsibility for debts incurred by the business.

## Liquidation

The process of converting property and **securities** into cash. When a company is dissolved or closed down, cash remaining after sale of its **assets** and payment of all indebtedness is distributed to the **shareholders**, beginning with the **preferred** shareholders and ending with the **common** shareholders.

## Liquidity

This refers to how easily **securities** can be bought or sold in the market. A security is liquid when there are enough units outstanding to allow large transactions without a substantial change in price. Liquidity is one of the most important characteristics of a good market. Liquidity also refers to how easily investors can convert their securities into cash and refers to a corporation's cash position, i.e. how much the value of **current assets** exceed **current liabilities**.

## Listed Stock

The **stock** of a company which is traded on a **stock exchange**. Companies pay fees to the exchange to be listed and must abide by the rules and regulations set out by the exchange to maintain listing privileges.

## Listing Statement

A **stock exchange** document published when a company's **shares** are accepted for listing. It provides basic information on the company, its business, management, **assets**, **capitalization** and financial status.

## Load

A charge added to **mutual funds** which covers sales **commissions** and all other costs of distribution. The load, usually a percentage of the money invested in the fund, may be charged as a front-end, on the purchase of the fund, or as a back-end, when the fund is sold or redeemed.

## Locked In

When an investor has a profit on a **security** owned, but does not sell because of either the absence of a market or some legal restriction on the sale of the security. Also refers to an investor holding a security which has declined below the purchase price who cannot sell without incurring a loss.

## Long

Term used to signify ownership of **securities**. "I am long 100 BCE common" means that the investor owns 100 **common shares** of BCE Inc.

## Long-Term Bond or Debenture

A **bond** or **debenture** maturing in more than 10 years.

## Low

This is the lowest price paid for a **stock** during a certain period. For example, the low for the day was $15, but the low for the year was $7.50.

# Mm

## Major Trend

Underlying price trend prevailing in a market despite temporary declines or rallies.

## Managed Account

This is similar to a **discretionary** account where a client has given specific written authorization to a partner, director or qualified portfolio manager of an **investment dealer** to select **securities** and execute trades, but on a continuing basis and for a fee. Managed accounts can be solicited whereas discretionary accounts are opened as a matter of convenience to clients who are ill or out of the country.

## Manipulation

The illegal practice of buying or selling a **security** for the purpose of creating a false or misleading appearance of active trading, or for the purpose of raising or depressing the price to induce purchases or sales by others.

## Margin Account

A client account where he or she uses credit from the **investment dealer** to buy a **security**. The client needs to deposit a "margin" amount with the balance being advanced by the investment dealer against acceptable **collateral** such as investments. The investment dealer can make a "margin call" and demand that the client deposit more money or securities when the value of the account falls below a certain level. If the client does not meet the margin call, the dealer can sell the securities in the margin account at a possible loss to cover the balance owed. The client is also charged interest on the money borrowed from the investment dealer for the purchase of the securities.

### Market Maker

An authorized **trader** employed by an **investment dealer** who is required by the applicable **self-regulatory organizations** to maintain reasonable **liquidity** in **securities** markets by making **firm bids or offers** for one or more designated securities.

### Market Order

An order placed to buy or sell a **security** immediately at the best current price.

### Market Out Clause

A clause in an **underwriting** agreement allowing the underwriter to cancel the agreement without penalty for certain specified reasons, such as the **issue** becoming unsaleable due to an unexpected change in **securities** markets, or in the affairs of the company whose securities are being underwritten.

### Market Price

The most recent price at which a **security** transaction took place.

### Marketable

Easily bought or sold.

### Material Change

A change in the affairs of a company that is expected to have a significant effect on the market value of its **securities** – such as a change in the nature of the business, a change in the Board of Directors or the principal officers, a change in the **share** ownership of the company that could affect control, or the acquisition or disposition of any securities in another company. A material change must be reported to the applicable **self-regulatory organization**.

## Maturity

The date on which a loan or a **bond** or **debenture** comes due and is to be paid off.

## Medium-Term Bond or Debenture

A **bond** or **debenture** which matures in more than three years, but less than 10.

## Member Firm

An **investment dealer** which owns a seat on a particular **stock exchange** or is a member of the **Investment Dealers Association of Canada**.

## Merger

The act of one company permanently joining another to become one company.

## Minority Interest

This appears on consolidated financial statements where the parent company's figures are combined with those of its **subsidiaries**. Even if the parent company owns less than 100% of a subsidiary's **stock**, all of the subsidiary's **assets** and **liabilities** are combined in the **consolidated financial statements**. To compensate, the part not owned by the parent company is minority interest and is shown as a liability on the **balance sheet** and deducted in the **earnings statement**.

## Monetary Policy

A policy followed by the federal government through the **Bank of Canada** for controlling credit and the money supply in the economy. The policy will vary according to the anti-inflationary or job-creating results the government primarily desires to achieve.

## Money Market

That part of the **capital market** in which short-term financial obligations are bought and sold. These include federal government **treasury bills**, short term

Government of Canada **bonds**, **commercial paper**, **bankers' acceptances** and **guaranteed investment certificates**. Longer term **securities**, when their term shortens to three years, are also traded in the money market.

## Mortgage

A contract specifying that certain property is pledged as security for a loan. The money is to be repaid in installments which usually combine **principal** and **interest** payments.

## Mortgage Backed Securities

Similar to **bonds**, these **securities** are backed by a share in a pool of home **mortgages** insured under the National Housing Act. The securities pay **interest** and a part of the **principal** each month and, if home owners prepay their mortgages, may pay out additional amounts of principal before normal **maturity**. They trade in the bond market at prices reflecting current interest rates.

## Mutual Funds

These are open-end funds that are not listed for trading on a **stock exchange** and are issued by companies which use their **capital** to invest in other companies. Mutual funds sell their own new **shares** to investors and buy back their old shares upon **redemption**. **Capitalization** is not fixed and normally shares are issued as people want them.

# Nn

## NASD

The National Association of Securities Dealers, Inc. This is the American **self-regulatory organization** of the **securities** industry responsible for the regulation of **NASDAQ** and the **over-the-counter** markets.

## NASDAQ

The National Association of Securities Dealers Automated Quotations System, the electronic, **over-the-counter**, screen-based communications system used by the second largest U.S. securities market.

## Negative Pledge Provision

A protective provision written into the trust deed of a company's **debenture** issue, providing that no subsequent mortgage bond issue may be secured by all or part of the company's **assets**, unless at the same time the company's debentures are similarly secured.

## Negotiable

A certificate that is transferable by delivery and which, in the case of a registered **certificate**, has been duly endorsed and guaranteed. Transferable from one party to another.

## Net Asset Value

Total **assets** of a corporation less its **liabilities**. Also referred to as **shareholders' equity**.

## Net Change

The change in the price of a **security** from the closing price on one day to the closing price on the following trading day. For example, ABC traded yesterday at 25⅝ and today it closed at 27. The net change is 1⅜. In the case of a **stock** which is entitled to a **dividend** one day, but is traded **ex-dividend** the next, the dividend is not considered in computing the change. The same applies to **stock splits**. A stock selling at $100 the day before a two-for-one split and trading the next day at $50 would be considered unchanged.

## Net Earnings

That part of a company's profits remaining after all expenses and taxes have been paid and out of which **dividends** may be paid.

## Net Sales

Gross sales less any applicable excise taxes, returns, allowances and discounts or rebates given to customers.

## Net Worth

The difference between a company's total **assets** less its total **liabilities**. Also referred to as **shareholders' equity**.

## New Issue

A **stock** or **bond issue** sold by a company for the first time. Proceeds may be used to retire **outstanding securities** of the company, or be used for a new plant or equipment or for additional **working capital**. New **debt** issues are also offered by governments.

## No Par Value (n.p.v.)

**Common stock** that has no stated **face value**. This is the usual practice in Canada so it is assumed and not always stated on the **share certificate**.

## Nominal Interest Rate

The stated **interest** rate, which does not take inflation into consideration.

## Non-Cumulative

A **preferred dividend** which does not accumulate if unpaid.

## Note

An unsecured promise to pay, such as a promissory note.

# Oo

## Odd Lot

A number of **shares** equalling less than a **board lot**, the regular **trading unit** decided upon by the particular **stock exchange**. Also, an amount less than the **par value** of one trading unit on the **over-the-counter** market.

## Off-the-Board

This term refers to transactions made **over-the-counter** in unlisted **securities**, or, in a special situation, to a transaction involving a block of **listed stock** which is not executed on a recognized **stock exchange**.

## Offer

An offer is the same as an **ask**, which is the lowest price at which a person is willing to sell a **security**. This is opposed to a **bid**, which is the highest price at which a person is willing to buy a security.

## Of Record

**Shareholders of record** are those who appear on the company's books or records as of a certain date. If, for example, a company announces that it will pay a **dividend** to shareholders of record January 15, every shareholder whose name appears on the company's books on that day will be sent a dividend cheque from the company.

## Open-End or Mutual Fund Investment Company

This is a company which uses its **capital** to invest in other companies. Open-end, or **mutual funds**, sell their own new **shares** to investors, buy back their old shares, and are not listed for trading on a **stock exchange**.

Open-end funds get their name because their **capitalization** is not fixed and they normally issue more shares as people want them.

## Open Order

An order to buy or sell a **security** at a specified price which is valid until executed or cancelled.

## Open Outcry

Verbal **bids** and **offers** made on the trading floors of **stock exchanges**. This method of public auction is disappearing as stock exchanges become automated.

## Option

An investor who purchases an option has the right, but not the obligation, to buy or sell certain **securities** at a specified price within a specified time. A **put option** gives the holder the right to sell the security, a **call option** gives the right to buy the security.

## Option Eligible Securities

**Securities** which meet the eligibility criteria as **underlying** securities for **put** and **call options** on a **stock exchange**.

## Option Holder

The buyer of either a **call** or **put option**.

## Option Premium

This is the price of an **option**. It is the amount of money that the **option holder** pays for the rights and the **option writer** receives for the obligations granted by the option.

## Option Writer

The seller of either a **call** or **put option**. The option writer receives payment, called a **premium**, and is obligated to buy or sell the **underlying security** at a specified price, within a certain period of time, if called upon to do so.

## Out-of-the-Money Option

A **call option** is out-of-the-money if its **exercise** or **strike price** is above the current **market price** of the **underlying security**. A **put option** is out-of-the-money if its exercise or strike price is below the current market price of the underlying security.

## Out-of-Line

A **security** which appears to be selling too low or too high in relation to comparable issues.

## Outstanding Shares

**Securities** that have been **issued** and sold to **shareholders** are referred to as outstanding.

## Over-the-Counter (OTC)

A **securities** market made up of dealers who make trades over the telephone and/or computer. It is also called "unlisted market," "street market" and "between or inter-dealer market." Almost all **bonds** and **debentures**, as well as some **stocks**, are traded over-the-counter in Canada.

# Pp

## Paper

A short-term **negotiable debt security** or promise to pay.

## Paper Profit

A profit on a **security** which has not been taken. Paper profits become realized profits only when the security is sold. A paper loss is the opposite to this. An example of a paper profit would be the purchase of ABC at $25. It is now trading at $27, so the paper profit is $2 per share.

## Par Value

The stated **face value** of a **bond** or, in the case of **stock**, an amount assigned by the company's charter and expressed as a dollar amount per **share**. Par value of **common stock** usually has no relationship to the current market value and so **no par value** stock is issued. Par value of **preferred stock** is significant, however, as it indicates the dollar amount of **assets** each preferred share would be entitled to in the event of **liquidation** of the company.

## Pari Passu

This means "in equal proportion." It usually refers to equally ranking **issues** of a company's **preferred shares**.

## Participating Feature

This applies to some **preferred stocks** which, in addition to a fixed rate of **dividend**, also share in the earnings of the company and may receive additional dividends over and above their specified dividend rate.

## Penny Stocks

Low-priced speculative **issues** of **stock** selling at less than $1.00 a share.

## Piggy Back Warrants

Some **warrants** entitle the holder to acquire **shares** plus additional warrants at a later date. The warrants that are received upon the **exercise** of the initial warrants are known as piggy back warrants.

## Points

Points apply to **security** prices. In the case of **shares**, one point indicates $1.00 per share. For **bonds** and **debentures**, one point means 1% of **par value**. Par value is almost universally 100 for bonds.

## Poison Pill

A corporate provision to combat hostile **takeovers**. When triggered, the poison pill allows **shareholders** to acquire additional **shares** at below **market price**, thereby increasing the number of shares **outstanding** and making the takeover prohibitively expensive. Such plans are relatively new in corporate Canada and are the subject of some controversy regarding whom they are designed to protect – the shareholders or the management.

## Pooling of Interest

This occurs when a company issues **treasury shares** for the **assets** of another company so that the latter becomes a division or **subsidiary** of the acquiring company. Subsequent accounts of the parent company are set up to include the **retained earnings** and assets at **book value** (subject to certain adjustments) of the acquired company.

## Portfolio

The entire combination of **securities** or investments an individual or institution holds. A portfolio can contain a variety of government and company **bonds**, **preferred** and **common stocks** from different businesses and other types of securities and **assets**.

## Preferred Stocks or Shares

A class of **stock** that entitles the owners to a stated dollar value per share in **liquidation** (paid after **bond**holders) and a fixed **dividend** paid ahead of the company's **common shares**. Preferred shares usually only have **voting rights** when a stated number of dividends have been missed. Preferred shares are generally considered income investments.

## Premium

**1.** The amount by which a **bond** or **preferred stock** may sell above its **par value**. In the case of a new issue of bonds or **stocks**, the premium is the amount the **market price** rises over the original selling price. **2.** The premium can also refer to the part of the **redemption price** of a bond or preferred stock that is in excess of **face value**, par value or market price. **3.** When referring to **options**, the premium is the price paid by the buyer of an option contract to a seller.

## Price-Earnings Ratio or PE Multiple

This is a **common stock**'s current **market price** divided by annual per share earnings. This ratio is a short way of saying that a **share** is selling at so many times its actual or anticipated annual earnings. A price-earnings ratio is one tool used to compare one share to another.

## Primary Offering or Primary Market

The original sale of any **new issue** of a company's **securities**.

## Prime Rate

The **interest** rate chartered banks charge to their most credit-worthy borrowers.

## Principal

A dealer buying or selling **securities** for his or her own account. The term "principal" can also refer to a person's **capital** or to the **face value** of a bond.

## Prior Preferred

A **preferred stock** which in the **liquidation** of the issuing company would rank ahead of other classes of preferred shares as to **asset** and **dividend** entitlement.

## Private Placements

The **underwriting** of a **security** and its sale to a few buyers, usually **institutional**, in large amounts. No formal **prospectus** is needed to be prepared in this instance as the buyers are considered to be sophisticated.

## Pro Forma

When a **new issue** is being planned for distribution, the corporation issuing the **security** must tell the suppliers of the new **capital** how they intend on spending the money received from the sale of the securities. The corporation publishes a pro forma **balance sheet** which integrates the new pool of money into their current operation. This shows the **shareholders** how the corporation would have spent the money if they had it on the day the pro forma balance sheet was created.

## Pro Rata

This means "in proportion to." For example, a **dividend** is a pro rata payment because the amount of dividend each **shareholder** receives is in proportion to the number of **shares** he or she owns.

## Profit Taking

Selling **securities** to take a profit. The process of converting **paper profits** into cash.

## Program Trading

A sophisticated computerized trading strategy whereby a portfolio manager attempts to earn a profit from the price **spreads** between a **portfolio** of **equities** similar or identical to those underlying a designated stock index, e.g. the Standard & Poor's 500 Index, and the price at which **futures contracts** (or their **options**) on the index trade in financial futures markets.

## Prospectus

A legal document which describes the **securities** being offered for sale to the public. These documents usually disclose pertinent information concerning the company's operations, securities, management and purpose of the offering. The prospectus must be prepared in accordance with requirements of the applicable provincial **securities commissions**.

## Proxy

Written authorization given by a **shareholder** to someone else, who does not necessarily need to be a shareholder, to represent him or her and vote at a shareholders' meeting.

## Prudent Portfolio Rule

In some provinces the law requires that a **trustee** may only invest in a **security** if it is one which an ordinary prudent person would buy if he or she were investing for the benefit of other people for whom he or she felt morally bound to provide. Some provinces apply both this rule and the rule under **legal investment**, where a list of specific securities has been designated.

## Purchase Fund

A fund set up by a company to retire, through purchases in the market, a specified amount of its **outstanding preferred shares** or **debt**. Purchases are made at or below a stipulated price.

## Push-out

During a **stock split**, a push-out occurs when new **shares** are forwarded directly to the registered holders of old **share certificates**, without the holders having to surrender these old shares. Both old and new shares have equal value.

## Put Options

An **option** which gives the holder the right, but not the obligation, to sell a fixed amount of a certain **stock** at a specified price within a specified time. Puts are purchased by those who think a stock may go down in price.

# Qq

## Quotation or Quote

The highest **bid** to buy and the lowest **offer** to sell a **security** at a given time. For example, a quote of $45\frac{1}{4}$ - $45\frac{1}{2}$ means that $45\frac{1}{4}$ is the highest price a buyer will pay and $45\frac{1}{2}$ is the lowest price a seller will accept.

# Rr

## Rally

A brisk rise in the general price level of the market or in an individual **stock**.

## Reaction

A temporary price weakness in a **security** following a price upswing.

## Real Estate Investment Trust (REIT)

An investment vehicle that invests funds on behalf of its investors in real estate-related investments such as construction loans, **mortgages**, land and real estate company **securities**.

## Real Interest Rate

The nominal rate of **interest** minus the percentage change in the **Consumer Price Index**, or the rate of inflation.

## Record Date

The day a company sets as the last day people can buy **stock** and receive such things as **dividends** or **rights**. These people are called **stockholders of record**.

## Red Herring

A preliminary **prospectus**, so-called because certain information is printed in red ink around the border of the front page. It does not contain all the information found in the final prospectus. Its purpose is to ascertain the extent of public interest in an **issue** while it is being reviewed by a **securities commission**.

## Redemption

The purchase of **securities** by the issuing company from the holder, at a time and price stipulated in the original terms of the securities. The redemption price is the price at which **debt** securities or **preferred shares** may be redeemed at the option of the issuing company.

## Refinancing or Refunding

When new **securities** are sold by a government or a company and the money is used to pay off existing loans. The object may be to save **interest** costs, extend the **maturity** of the loan, or both.

## Registered Pension Plan (RPP)

A RPP is a trust registered with Revenue Canada and established by a company to provide pension benefits for its employees when they retire. Both employee and employer contributions to the plan are tax deductible.

## Registered Representative

Now more commonly referred to as an **investment advisor**. This is a person employed by an **investment dealer** who provides investment advice to clients and executes trades on their behalf in **securities** and other investment products. Investment advisors must attain set educational qualifications, follow certain rules and regulations and be registered by the **securities commission** of the province in which he or she works.

## Registered Retirement Income Fund (RRIF)

A RRIF is a tax deferral vehicle available to **Registered Retirement Savings Plan** (RRSP) holders who de-register their plans. The plan holder invests the withdrawn RRSP funds in the RRIF and each year must withdraw and pay income tax on a set fraction of the total assets in the fund.

## Registered Retirement Savings Plan (RRSP)

A vehicle available to individuals to defer tax on a specified amount of money to be used for retirement. The holder invests money in one or more of a variety of investment vehicles which are held in trust under the plan. Income tax is deferred until the money (the amount originally deposited plus any **interest** or **dividends** made on that money) is withdrawn at retirement. RRSPs can be converted into **Registered Retirement Income Funds**.

## Registered Security

A **security** recorded on the books of a company in the name of the owner. It can only be transferred when the securities **certificate** is endorsed in that name and the certificate is forwarded to the **transfer agent**. Registered **debt** securities may be registered as to **principal** only or fully registered. In the case of fully registered debt securities, **interest** is paid by cheque rather than by **coupons** attached to the certificate.

## Registered Tax Deferral Savings Plans

Government-approved savings plans such as **Registered Pension Plans**, **Registered Retirement Savings Plans** and **Registered Retirement Income Funds**, in which funds contributed by individuals are tax-deductible within certain limits and investment earnings accumulate in the plans on a tax-deferred basis until de-registration or **maturity** of the plans.

## Registrar

Usually a trust company appointed by a company to manage the issuance and registration of **securities certificates**.

## Registration

**1.** The process of **securities** registration involves filing a **prospectus** with the **securities administrators** as required under the Securities Act of each province in which the securities will be offered. **2. Investment**

**dealers** and sales staff involved in the investment business must be registered with the applicable **self-regulatory organization**. Before registration is allowed, basic standards must be met, such as minimum **capital** requirements for a firm and minimum educational qualifications for personnel.

## Reporting Issuer

A corporation that has **issued** and **outstanding securities** held by the public and is subject to the **continuous disclosure** requirements of **securities administrators**.

## Repurchase Agreements

An agreement between a seller and a buyer, usually in government **securities**, in which the seller agrees to buy back the security at a later date.

## Resistance

Used in **technical analysis** to describe a price level that a **security** has difficulty reaching.

## Restricted Shares

**Shares** that have limited **voting rights** or in some cases, no voting rights. These shares participate in a company's earnings and **assets** in **liquidation** as **common shares** do and are sometimes referred to as restricted common shares. Restricted shares may not command the same **market price** as voting common shares of the same company since they do not have voting rights.

## Retained Earnings

The cumulative total portion of annual earnings retained by a company after payment of all expenses and **dividends**. Can be considered money that the company puts back into its business for expansion, etc.

## Retractable

A feature which can be included in a **new debt issue** or **preferred share** which grants the holder the option, under specified conditions, to redeem the **security** on a stated date. This date would be prior to **maturity** in the case of a debt issue.

## Return

The income earned or a **capital gain** made on an investment.

## Reverse Split

The exchange of a greater number of a company's **shares** for a lesser number. For example, exchanging three shares for one. This results in a higher share price and less shares outstanding. This is also called a consolidation or a negative split.

## Right

The temporary privilege granted to a company's existing **common shareholders** to acquire additional **common shares** directly from the company at a stated price. The price is usually at a discount to the **market price** of the common stock on the day the rights are **issued**, and the rights only are good within a specified time period. Rights of **listed** companies trade on **stock exchanges** from the **ex rights** date until their expiry, so holders can either **exercise** the rights or they can sell them.

## Right of Rescission

The right of a purchaser of a **new issue** to withdraw from the purchase agreement within the specific province's applicable time limits if the **prospectus** contained an untrue statement or omitted a material fact.

## Right of Withdrawal

The right of a purchaser of a **new issue** to withdraw from the purchase agreement within two business days after receiving the **prospectus**.

## Risk

The future chance or probability of loss.

# S

## Scrip

A **certificate** exchangeable for cash before a specified date, after which it may have no value. Usually issued for fractions of **shares** in connection with a **stock dividend** or **split** or in a reorganization of a company. For example, a one-for-three stock dividend would result in many **shareholders** being entitled to a fraction of a share ($^1/_3$ or $^2/_3$) for which scrip would be issued instead of an actual stock certificate.

## Seat

The traditional term for membership on a **stock exchange**. An **investment dealer** would buy a seat on the exchange and one employee would be designated as the seat holder.

## SEC

The Securities and Exchange Commission, a federal body established by the United States Congress as a national U.S. regulatory authority. In Canada there is no national regulatory authority because **securities** legislation is provincially administered.

## Secondary Distribution or Secondary Offering

The redistribution of a block of **stock** after it has been initially sold by the issuing company. Usually a large block of shares is involved (e.g. from the settlement of an estate) and these are offered to the public at a fixed price, set in relationship to the stock's **market price**.

## Secondary Market

Secondary markets are the **stock exchanges** and the **over-the-counter** market. **Securities** are first **issued** as a **primary offering** to the public. When the securities are traded from that first holder to another, the issues trade in these secondary markets.

## Securities

Transferable **certificates** of ownership of investment products such as **notes**, **bonds**, **stocks**, **futures contracts** and **options**.

## Securities Administrator

A general term referring to the provincial regulatory authority (e.g. **securities commission**) responsible for administering provincial securities acts.

## Securities Advisor

A person or firm registered with applicable **securities commissions** to generally advise the public on **securities**, often through publications.

## Securities Commission

Each province has a **securities commission or administrator** which oversees the provincial securities act. This act is a set of laws and regulations which set down the rules under which **securities** may be **issued** and traded.

## Securitization

**1.** The development of markets for a variety of **debt** instruments that permit the ultimate borrower to bypass the banks and other deposit-taking institutions and to borrow directly from lenders. **2.** In a narrow sense it also refers to the process of converting loans of various sorts into marketable **securities** by packaging the loans into pools and then selling **shares** of ownership in the pool itself.

## Self-Regulatory Organizations (SROs)

Many important rules governing **securities** industry practices and standards in Canada are set by the self-regulatory organizations, which include the Vancouver, Alberta and Toronto Stock Exchanges, the Montreal Exchange and the **Investment Dealers Association of Canada**. Many of the regulatory and compliance functions have been delegated to the SROs by the provincial **securities administrators**.

## Selling Group

**Investment dealers** who assist a **banking group** in marketing **a new issue** of **securities** in order to obtain wide distribution. These dealers do not assume financial responsibility for the **underwriting** of the issue as the banking group does.

## Senior Bond Issue

A corporate **bond issue** which has priority over other bonds as to its claim on the company's **assets** and earnings. An example is a first mortgage bond.

## Senior Debt

A senior debt issue ranks before other **issues** in terms of claims on **assets** in the event of a company break-up. For example, senior bonds rank before junior bonds, which rank before senior **debentures**, which rank before junior debentures, etc.

## Serial Bond or Debenture

A **bond** or **debenture issue** in which a predetermined amount of the **principal** becomes due and payable each year.

## Settlement Date

The date on which a **security** buyer must pay for his or her purchase, or a seller must deliver the securities he or she has sold. In Canada, investors have three days to pay for a purchase or, if selling, three days to turn in the securities **certificate** if it is in their possession.

### Shareholder or Stockholder

Someone who owns **preferred** or **common shares** of a company.

### Shareholders' Equity

Ownership interest of **common** and **preferred stockholders** in a company. It is also the difference between the **assets** and **liabilities** of a company, which is sometimes called **net worth**, or just "equity."

### Shareholder of Record

A **shareholder** whose name is registered in the records of a company whose **shares** he or she holds. **Dividend** payments and **rights issues** are announced as being payable to shareholders of record.

### Shares or Stocks

These two terms are used interchangeably. **Certificates** representing ownership in a corporation and the appropriate claim on the corporation's earnings and **assets**.

### Short Selling

The sale of a **security** which the seller does not own. This is a speculative practice done in the belief that the price of a **stock** is going to fall and the seller will then be able to cover the sale by buying the security back at a lower price. The profit would be the difference between the initial selling price and the subsequent purchase price. It is illegal for a seller not to declare a short sale at the time of placing the order.

### Short-term Bond

A **bond** or **debenture maturing** within three years.

### Short-term Debt

Company borrowings repayable within one year that appear in the current **liabilities** section of the company's **balance sheet**. The most common short-term debt items are bank advances or loans, **notes** payable, **debentures** and **bonds** due within one year.

## Sinking Fund

A fund set up by a company to retire, over a period of time, the major part of a **preferred share issue**, or a **debt** issue prior to **maturity**. The fund helps to "pay off" the debt issue over the term of the issue and can be compared to principal payments made by a **mortgage** holder. Even though the issue is **outstanding** until maturity, the small incremental payments made under a sinking fund can make the maturity of the bond issue less onerous on the company. Instead of having to re-fund the entire issue, there may only be a small outstanding balance. A sinking fund security is attractive to investors as there is more assurance that the debt will be repaid on maturity.

## Speculator

A speculator is one who is prepared to accept calculated **risks** in the marketplace for attractive potential **returns**. A speculator's objective is usually short to medium term **capital gain**, whereas regular income and safety of **principal** are the prime goals of the conservative investor.

## Spread

**1.** The gap between the **bid** and **ask** prices in the **quotation** for a **security**. **2.** The term can also be applied to certain strategies for **options** and **commodities** where the investor is trading on the differences in prices between two related securities.

## Statement of Changes in Financial Position

A financial statement which provides information as to how a company generated and spent its cash during the year. It links the company's **balance sheets** for two successive years and provides a summary of the incoming and outgoing movement of a company's funds for the period. It explains changes in **working capital** (current **assets** less current **liabilities**) from one year to the next.

## Statement of Material Facts

A document presenting the relevant facts about a company and compiled in connection with an **underwriting** or **secondary distribution** of its **shares.** It is used only when the shares underwritten or distributed are listed on a recognized **stock exchange** and takes the place of a **prospectus** in such cases.

## Stockholder or Shareholder

Someone who owns **preferred** or **common shares** of a company.

## Stock Consolidation

The opposite of a **stock split**. A number of existing **shares** are combined into a smaller number of shares, ie. turning every three shares into one.

## Stock Dividend

**Dividends** paid to **shareholders** in shares of **stock** rather than cash.

## Stock Exchange or Stock Market

An organized marketplace where buyers and sellers are brought together to buy and sell **stocks** and must follow certain rules, regulations and guidelines.

## Stock Index

An indicator used to measure and report value changes in a specific group of **stocks**. For example, the TSE 300 Index measures 300 stocks with the greatest market **capitalization** of all the companies listed on the Toronto Stock Exchange.

## Stock Savings Plan

Some provinces, such as Quebec, Nova Scotia, Saskatchewan and Newfoundland offer stock savings plans which allow individuals in those provinces a deduction or tax credit for provincial income tax purposes. The credit or deduction is a percentage figure based on the value of investment in certain prescribed vehicles.

## Stock Split

Division of a company's **outstanding common shares** into a larger number of common shares. A three-for-one split by a company with one million shares outstanding would result in three million shares outstanding. Each holder of 100 shares before the three-for-one split would have 300 shares after the split, but his or her proportionate equity in the company would remain the same – each unit would just be smaller.

## Stocks or Shares

These two terms are used interchangeably. **Certificates** representing ownership in a corporation and the appropriate claim on the corporation's earnings and **assets**.

## Stock Symbol

An unique three or four letter symbol assigned to a **security** trading on a **stock exchange**. For example, Hollinger Inc. is listed as HLG on the Toronto Stock Exchange.

## Stop Loss and Stop Buy Orders

Orders for certain **securities** when the price of a **stock** rises or falls to a specified price. A stop loss order is an order to sell when the price of the stock declines to, or below, a stated price. The purpose of this is to reduce the amount of loss that might occur. A stop buy order is an order to buy a stock when the price rises to a certain level. This is given by a person who has sold a security **short** and is an attempt to reduce loss or protect a profit should the price rise unexpectedly.

## Street Certificate or "Street Name"

Most people who own **securities** today do not physically have possession of the **stock** or **bond certificates**. Their securities are kept on their behalf by their **investment dealer**, which is called keeping securities in "street name." All **interest** payments and **dividends** are passed onto the client by crediting their account with the dealer.

## Strike Price

The price at which the **underlying stock** of a **call option** can be purchased, or the price at which the underlying stock of a **put option** can be sold. Also referred to as the **exercise price**.

## Strip Bonds or Zero Coupon Bonds

Usually high quality federal or provincial government **bonds** originally issued in **bearer** form, where some or all of the **interest coupons** have been detached. The bond **principal** and any remaining coupons trade separately from the strip of detached coupons, both at substantial **discounts** from **par**.

## Stripped Debentures

**Debentures** which have been separated from other **securities**, such as **warrants**, which were originally issued together as a **unit**.

## Subject Bid, Subject Offer

A **bid** or **offer** made for a **security** that indicates the buyer's interest, in the case of a bid, or the seller's interest, in the case of an offer, but does not commit the buyer or seller to the purchase or sale of the security at that price or time.

## Subsidiary

A company which is controlled by another company, usually by owning the majority of the first company's **shares**.

## Surplus

**Contributed surplus** is a **balance sheet** figure which originates from sources other than earnings, such as the initial sale of **stock** above **par value**. Earned surplus, or **retained earnings**, is the amount of accumulated earnings retained in the business after the payment of all expenses and **dividends**.

## Surtax

An additional income tax over and above the regular income tax amount. Usually used as a temporary measure to raise funds for short-term needs.

## Sweetener

A feature included in the terms of a **new issue** of **debt** or **preferred shares** to make the issue more attractive to initial investors. Examples of sweeteners include **warrants**, or **convertible**, **extendible** or **retractable** features.

## Switching

Selling one **security** and buying another.

## Syndicate

A group of **investment dealers** who **underwrite** and distribute a new issue of **securities** or a large block of an **outstanding issue**.

# t

## Takeover Bid

An offer made to **security** holders of a company to purchase their voting securities which, together with the offering individual's already owned securities, will total over 20% of the **outstanding** voting securities of the company. For federally incorporated companies, the equivalent requirement is more than 10% of the outstanding voting shares of the target company.

## Tax Bracket

Although income tax is paid by most wage or income earners, the rate of income tax paid increases as income exceeds certain amounts, called brackets.

## Tax Credit

Tax credits reduce taxes payable to the same extent for all taxpayers, regardless of their income level and marginal tax rate. Deductions from taxable income, however, are more valuable as your income and tax rate increases.

## Tax Shelter

This is an investment that offers tax savings in some form, such as immediate deductions, credits or income deferral.

## T-Bill

Common term for a government **treasury bill**, which is a short-term government **debt** issue.

## Technical Analysis

A method of **market** and **security** analysis that studies investor attitudes and psychology as revealed in charts of **stock** price movements and trading volumes. This analysis may be used to assess possible future price action.

## Term Deposit Receipt

A deposit instrument most commonly available from chartered banks requiring a minimum investment at a predetermined rate of **interest** for a stated term. The interest rate varies according to the amount invested and the term to **maturity**, but is competitive with comparable alternative investments. A reduced interest rate usually applies if funds are withdrawn prior to maturity.

## Thin Market

A market in which there are comparatively few **bids** to buy or **offers** to sell, or both. The phrase may apply to a single **security** or to the entire **stock market**. In a thin market, price fluctuations between transactions are usually larger than when the market is **liquid**. A thin market in a particular stock may reflect lack of interest in that **issue**, or a limited supply of the **stock**.

## Time Limit Order

A client order that specifies the time during which it can be executed.

## Time Value or Extrinsic Value

The amount that the current **market price** of a **right**, **warrant** or **option** exceeds its **intrinsic value**. Intrinsic value is the amount by which the market price of a **security** exceeds the price at which the warrant, right or option may be **exercised**. The intrinsic value of a **put** is calculated as the amount by which the market price of the **underlying** security is below the **exercise price**.

## Timely Disclosure

The obligation for companies to promptly release to the news media any favorable or unfavorable corporate information which is of a material nature. This obligation is imposed by the **securities administrators** on companies. Broad dissemination of this news allows all investors to trade the company's **securities** with the same knowledge about the company as **insiders**.

## Trader

**1.** Employee of an **investment dealer** who executes buy and sell orders for the dealer and its clients either on a **stock exchange** or the **over-the-counter** market. **2.** The term is also used to describe a client who buys and sells frequently with the objective of short-term profit.

## Trading Halt

Suspension of trading in a **security** while material news from the issuer is being spread. A trading halt gives all investors equal opportunity to hear the news and make any appropriate trade decisions.

## Trading Units

Different **par values** make up trading units for the **over-the-counter** market. For example, one trading unit of Government of Canada **treasury bills** is $250,000 par value, while one trading unit of provincial **bonds** and guarantees is $25,000 par value.

## Transaction Date

The date on which the purchase or sale of a **security** takes place.

## Transfer Agent

A trust company appointed by a company to keep a record of the names, addresses and number of **shares** held by its **shareholders**. Frequently the transfer agent also distributes **dividend** cheques.

## Treasury Bills

Short-term government **debt**, usually issued in **trading units** of $250,000 and sold chiefly to large **institutional** investors. Treasury bills do not pay **interest** but are sold at a **discount** and **mature** at **par** (100). The difference between the purchase price and par at maturity represents the purchaser's income in lieu of interest. In Canada such gain is taxed as interest income in the purchaser's hands.

## Treasury Shares

**Authorized** but unissued stock of a company, or previously **issued** shares that have been re-acquired by the corporation.

## Trustee

**1.** Usually a trust company appointed by the company to protect the **security** behind the company's **bonds** and to make certain that all covenants of the trust deed relating to the bonds are honored. **2.** A person who holds property and securities in trust for another person.

# U u

## Underlying Securities

The specific **security** that is bought or sold by exercising an **option**.

## Underwriting

The purchase for resale of a **security issue** by one or more **investment dealers** or "underwriters." The formal agreements pertaining to such a transaction are called "underwriting agreements."

## Unit

Two or more corporate **securities** (such as **preferred shares** and **warrants**) offered for sale to the public at a single, combined price.

## Unlisted

A **security** not listed on a **stock exchange** but traded on the **over-the-counter** market.

# V v

## Venture Capital

Money raised by companies to finance new, **risky** ventures.

## Volatility

The rate of change in the price of a **security** over a given time.

## Volume

The amount of **shares** bought and sold on a **stock exchange**.

## Voting Right

The **stockholder**'s right to vote in the affairs of the company. Most **common shares** have one vote each and **preferred stock** usually only has the right to vote when its **dividends** are in **default**. The right to vote may be delegated by the stockholder to another person, called voting by **proxy**. Voting rights give the stockholder a say in the company's affairs and such rights can increase the value of the stock.

## Voting Trust

A device to place the control of a company in the hands of certain managers for a given period of time, or until certain results have been achieved. This is done by **shareholders** surrendering their **voting rights** to a **trustee** for a specified period of time.

# W

## Warrant

A **certificate** giving the holder the right to purchase **securities** at a stipulated price within a specified time limit. Warrants are usually issued along with a **new issue** of securities as an inducement or **sweetener** to investors to buy the new issue.

## Working Capital

Current **assets** of a company minus its current **liabilities**. This figure shows the company's **liquidity** and ability to meet its short-term **debts**.

## Working Capital Ratio

Current **assets** of a company divided by its current **liabilities**. This is a measure of a company's **liquidity**.

## Working Control

Theoretically, ownership of 51% of a company's voting **stock** is necessary to exercise control. In practice, and this is particularly true in the case of a large corporation, effective control sometimes can be exerted through ownership, individually or by a group acting in concert, of less than 50%.

## Wrap Account

A type of fully **discretionary account** (in which a client has given specific written authorization to a partner, director or qualified portfolio manager of an **investment dealer** to select **securities** and execute trades for him or her). A single annual fee, based on the account's total **assets**, is charged instead of **commissions** and service charges being levied separately for each transaction. The account is then managed separately from all other wrap accounts, but is kept consistent with a model **portfolio** suitable to clients with similar objectives. This is also known as a wrap fee program.

# Yy

## Yield

This is the measure of the **return** on an investment and is shown as a percentage. A **stock** yield is calculated by dividing the annual **dividend** by the current **market price** of the stock. For example, a stock selling at $50 and with an annual dividend of $5.00 per share yields 10%. A **bond** yield is a more complicated calculation, involving annual **interest** payments plus **amortizing** the difference between its current market price and **par value** over the life of the bond.

## Yield Curve

A graphic representation of the relationship among **yields** of **bonds** of the same quality, but with different **maturities**.

## Yield to Maturity

The rate of **return** an investor receives if a fixed-income **security** is held to **maturity**.

# Z z

## Zero Coupon Bonds

Usually high quality federal or provincial government **bonds** originally issued in **bearer** form, where some or all of the **interest coupons** have been detached. The bond **principal** and any remaining coupons trade separately from the strip of detached coupons, both at substantial **discounts** from **par**. Also called **strip bonds**.

# Publications & courses available in English & French from the Investor Learning Centre

## How to Invest in Canadian Securities

Everything you want to know about investing is clearly presented in this straightforward but comprehensive guide. An invaluable investor's resource for more than 27 years, *How to Invest in Canadian Securities* explains the secrets of stocks, bonds, mutual funds, options and futures – all in a down-to-earth style that anyone can understand. The 245-page book contains a wealth of stock market wisdom gathered over the years by the respected Canadian Securities Institute, the official educator of Canada's brokerage industry.

## How to Start and Run an Investment Club for Fun & Learning

Learning about investing in the company of friends can be a lot of fun – especially when you're making money, too. This step-by-step Canadian guide explains everything from choosing the right mix of members to keeping track of club cash and tips on taxes. All of which will ensure the success of your club.

## What Every Canadian Should Know About Family Finance

Retirement planning, saving for your kids' education and income protection are key goals for many families. This plain-language book offers practical information and strategies to help make your plans a reality. It's for families at all different life stages, offering tips on credit management, mortgages, insurance, investments, pensions and income tax. It shows you how to measure and grow your family's net worth.

## The Investor's Handbook

If you're in a hurry to learn as much as you can about investing, then this comprehensive yet concise book is what you need. It offers invaluable reference information on a wide variety of securities, from mutual funds to plain vanilla bonds to structured derivative products. As a primer on investing, this book also provides tips on finding and working with a financial advisor and knowing how to troubleshoot problems.

## What Every Canadian Should Know About Mutual Funds

To get the most value out of mutual funds, you need to learn the three key styles used by the fund managers, and how to figure out the funds' risk-return profile. All of this is explained in a clear, engaging style in *What Every Canadian Should Know About Mutual Funds*. This book takes you through the steps so you end up with a portfolio of mutual funds that suits your needs. It's even got a chapter on alternatives to funds.

## What Every Canadian Should Know About Stocks

Straightforward and practical, *What Every Canadian Should Know About Stocks* subscribes to the best traditions of conservative buy-and-hold stock investing. You'll learn how to analyze a company's fundamentals using financial ratios, decipher technical charts and read the significance of key economic indicators. For long-term investors who want a prudent approach to picking stocks, this book's the ticket.

## Intelligent Investing Level 1 and 2.

You might be looking for an introduction to investing. Or maybe you want to develop your skills and confidence as a hands-on investor. *Intelligent Investing Level 1* is a six-session weekly seminar course designed to give novice investors a basic overview of investment principles, stocks, bonds and mutual funds, and practical information on how to start investing and planning for retirement. *Intelligent Investing Level 2* is an eight-session weekly seminar course aimed at graduates of Level 1. It's an advanced course offering the practical tools and knowledge you need to compare the investment merits of companies using financial ratios and technical analysis. Stock and bond investing strategies for good times and bad are explained, along with evaluating mutual fund performance and how to build and manage your portfolio.

Please refer to the latest *Intelligent Investing* brochure for a list of cities across Canada where these two seminar series are offered.

Investor
Learning
Centre
OF CANADA

The Canadian Securities Institute (CSI), which founded the ILC, is Canada's recognized leader in investment learning. Not-for-profit, independent and national, the CSI offers programs for people in all sectors of the financial services industry.

## The Canadian Securities Course™

The CSC is perhaps the best-known investment course in Canada. For people looking to start a career in financial services, the CSC is an essential qualification. From investment dealers to mutual fund companies, banks to financial planning and insurance firms, the CSC opens doors to many different careers. As well, many students who enrol in this course take it for their own personal investment knowledge or to enhance their current job.

## Professional Financial Planning

CSC graduates may enrol in Professional Financial Planning, the foremost financial planning course in Canada. Challenging, up-to-date and comprehensive, topics include budget and savings planning, residential mortgages, business and family law, insurance, investment management and tax, retirement and estate planning.

## Canadian Investment Management

Students in this prestigious program are deemed to be at the pinnacle of their investment industry studies. The in-depth curriculum analyses economic and institutional issues for portfolio managers and contains advanced material on the principles and applications of modern portfolio theory.

## Derivatives Fundamentals Course

This course is available for everyone and covers the basics of exchange-traded options, futures and over-the-counter derivatives. It is a prerequisite to the two CSI courses that are mandatory for people who wish to sell exchange-traded derivatives in Canada – the Options Licensing Course and the Futures Licensing Course.

These are just a few of the courses and programs available through the CSI. Flexible and self-study, CSI programs are open to anyone interested in investing. While many of our courses are mandatory for people wishing to become registered to work in the investment industry, people working in all areas of the financial services industry take our courses to enhance their careers.